The setting for this rowdy — perhaps a little bawdy at times — collection of hilarious yarns lies in Ash Fork, Arizona, a real town for which the term "jerkwater" was invented.

The characters, however, are pure fiction, coming from the imagination of Marshall Trimble, sometimes called Arizona's Will Rogers. Why, if these characters were real, the West would have been lost.

Trimble's cast includes rock doodlers, who are rock-digging reprobates usually residing at the butt end of jokes; a lawman whose badge was one point short of a circle; Rowena Lumpkin, the 400-pound Avon lady; a doctor who keeps office hours in a saloon; and a wise-cracking waitress named Crystal who beat Miss Yuma County for first runner-up in the Miss Arizona contest when the latter's tractor broke down during the talent competition.

Because he lived there in the 1940s and '50s, Trimble pokes fun at Ash Fork and its imaginary residents with impunity — that means that Ash Forkians let him get away with it because he's one of them.

The "bum steer" and "heifer" in this book's title are the co-stars of Trimble's story of the Looney brothers, Billy Bob and Jake, who buy Jubal Spitler's line that "the best way to start a cow ranch — short of rustling — is to buy a good bull and a fine heifer and let them go forth and multiply." Guess what the animal turns out to be?

Prepared by the Book Division of *Arizona Highways®* magazine, a monthly publication of the Arizona Department of Transportation.

Publisher — Nina M. La France
Managing Editor — Bob Albano
Associate Editor — Evelyn Howell
Art Director — Mary Winkelman Velgos
Production Director — Cindy Mackey

Printed in the United States
Library of Congress Catalog Number 99-63269
ISBN 0-916179-98-2

Never Give a Heifer a Bum Steer

BY MARSHALL TRIMBLE

ILLUSTRATIONS BY JACK GRAHAM

CAST OF CHARACTERS

Junior Frisby

He's devoted to catching
out-of-state speeders.

Rock Doodlers

They mostly reside at
the butt end of jokes.

Waddie Culpepper

There's a lot of giddy-up in this
cowboy's character.

Oracle Charlebois

He colors stories redder'n
a Navajo blanket.

Crystal LeDoux

She's more attractive than the
food at the Do Drop In café.

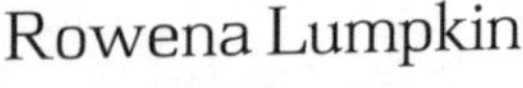

Rowena Lumpkin

She sings like a burro
with a bad cold.

Doc Pringle

He conducts his practice
mostly at the Arizona Bar.

CONTENTS

ABOUT THE AUTHOR

Marshall Trimble is a historian, folklorist, spinner of yarns, guitar picker, and singer. He blends those backgrounds in *Never Give a Heifer a Bum Steer.*

For a spell in the 1940s and '50s, he lived in Ash Fork, Arizona and uses that town for the setting of this collection of tall tales and jokes.

The entertainment side of him started in 1957, when he bought a used Gibson guitar for $5 and learned to play while listening to records by Elvis Presley, Buddy Holly, and Johnny Cash. A couple of years later, he attended a Kingston Trio concert and became hooked on folk music. In 1963, he joined a folksinging group called the Gin Mill Three. The boys cut four records and played Las Vegas, Reno, Lake Tahoe, and San Francisco. Hoping to present a cleaner image, a promoter changed the group's name to the Prairie Boys. After two years, the group broke up when one member got drafted and another got married.

Trimble returned to music in 1971 with a folk duo called Donnery and Rudd. "I don't know whether I was Donnery or Rudd," Trimble says. "We took the name from the label on a bottle of Cutty Sark Scotch."

In 1988, he wrote and recorded *Legends in Levis* as a tribute to cowboys of the Old West. Trimble's cowboy poetry has been published in national magazines such as *The American Cowboy*.

Along the way he added story-telling to his act and began writing books. He has written 17 books on Arizona and the West, including *The Law of the Gun*, published by *Arizona Highways*. A humor book, *It Always Rains After A Dry Spell*, was a national finalist for the Benjamin Franklin Award presented by the Publishers Marketing Association.

He has appeared on *Good Morning America, This Morning*, and has opened concerts for such acts as Waylon Jennings, the Oak Ridge Boys, and Jerry Lee Lewis.

Phoenix radio personality Pat McMahon described Trimble as " . . . the Will Rogers of Arizona."

The Arizona Historical Foundation said of Trimble: "Warm, witty, intelligent and always entertaining. . . . Marshall's homespun wit and unassuming demeanor often serve as a smokescreen to his incisive talents in scholarly arenas."

While studying the origins of folk music, Trimble took an interest in the history of the American West. In 1972, he began teaching Arizona and Southwest history at Scottsdale Community College and at the urging of his students, wrote *Arizona: A Panoramic History of a Frontier State*. The book, published by Doubleday, became a best seller.

INTRODUCTION

Idiots Give Rise to an Idiom

Old cowboy movies, with their tight-lipped, tight-trousered, hard-riding heroes, gave a lot of folks a romantically distorted picture of ranch life in the Old West. On the silver screen, the heroes spent most of their time in town helping other folks get out of a jam. For the hero, the movies always included a pretty school marm to rescue from a fate worse than death and some fool of a sidekick who said dumb things to make the hero look larger-than-life. Those shooting stars could fire hundreds of rounds from their six-shooters without reloading, never lose their hats in a fight, and get flesh wounds that healed by the next day. Their horses defied the laws of nature by never pooping in the streets.

Who can forget those scenes of Gene Autry riding through some remote desert wilderness, singing *I'm Back In The Saddle Again*, with a full orchestra backing him? An outlaw always hid up in the rocks drawing a bead on Gene but never firing until the song was over. I began to question the veracity of Westerns when I saw Roy Rogers jump out of a second-story window, land astride Trigger's back without flinching, and sing *Happy Trails* in a normal voice.

Since the West began, folks have been lured to the seemingly romantic life of the cowboy by one medium or another. First, it was the dime novel that drew them.

Some folks said that Harry Longabaugh learned about outlaws from reading dime novels. He headed west from his affluent eastern home and eventually started calling himself the Sundance Kid and hooked up with Butch Cassidy.

William Tattenbaum was drawn to Tombstone, Arizona, all the way from czarist Russia to live out his dream of being an outlaw. He arrived in town all decked out in fancy cowboy clothes. He had even gone to the trouble of carving notches on the handle of his six-gun.

Curly Bill and Tombstone's other outlaws were amused by this foreign greenhorn who spoke several languages and wanted to be called Russian Bill. Handsome and polite, he was too genteel to be a real outlaw, but nonetheless he tried.

Russian Bill stole a horse one day, and an angry posse immediately captured him. Posse members didn't see outlaws as romantic characters. For Bill, reality set in just before a mob hanged him in 1881 from the rafters of a restaurant in Shakespeare, New Mexico.

Later, Western movies romanticized ranch life, causing reasonably sane people to give up secure jobs and become ranchers.

The movies no doubt provided the inspiration for two Mississippi brothers named Billy Bob and Jake Looney to sell their pig farm outside Fool's Hollow and head west to become ranchers. Billy Bob and Jake had dreamed of becoming cowboys ever since they saw their first Western movie. Every Saturday afternoon they would head into town and watch their matinee heroes — Hoot Gibson, Buck Jones, Ken Maynard, and Tom Mix — chase desperados across the purple sage.

Those Hollywood cowboys spent most of their time in town helping beautiful damsels in distress, shooting up the bad guys, or just hanging out in the local saloon and raisin' hell. Ranching seemed like a fun and exciting life compared to the dreary job of raisin' hogs and plantin' butterbeans.

The Looney brothers arrived in Ash Fork, Arizona, in 1930, happier than a pup with three tails, with $4,000 cash and more plans than a politician. They stopped in at the town's social gathering place, the Arizona Bar, where they chanced to meet a salty old cowman named Jubal Spitler.

Jubal spotted those two redneck bubbas for a couple of greenhorns and convinced them that the best way to start a cow ranch — short of rustling — was to buy a good bull and a fine heifer and let them go forth and multiply.

"Heifers are a dime a dozen," Jubal said, "but a good bull is worth his weight in gold — or at least $4,000 cash."

After talking it over, the Looney brothers agreed to give Jubal their entire stake for a bull named Jeremiah. The old man agreed to throw in a heifer. For that price, he'd even throw in his ranch. That hardscrabble piece of malpai was dry as a church picnic and could grow nothing but tumbleweeds.

Jubal pocketed the Looneys' hard-earned cash and, following a time-honored business tradition in Arizona, headed for California. The only folks in two counties who didn't know Jeremiah was really a steer were the Looney brothers. Word got around real fast, and the locals couldn't wait for the young heifer to come in season.

When breeding time came, the Looney brothers led old Jeremiah into the pen and offered some words of encouragement. The look on that heifer's face, and Jeremiah's total bewilderment — along with the howls of laughter coming from the cowboys who'd gathered to watch the fun — were enough to convince even the Looney boys, who were dumb as a couple of fence posts, that they had been suckered.

As a result of this story, an addition was made to the American idiom: "Never give a heifer a bum steer." As a Mexican *dicho,* or saying, it's phrased, "No la di nunca una vaquilla, aun buey incapaz." In either language, understand that a heifer is a female animal and a steer is a neutered male.

A local country singer named Stem Hobgood wrote a song about it that was played on juke boxes all over town. It wasn't a big hit. In fact it never even made it beyond Ash Fork, thus depriving the citizens of the large cities nearby such as Peach Springs and Seligman from enjoying it.

CHAPTER 1

Biography of a Town Too Desolate to Die

Ash Fork, the Looney brothers' new hometown, became an important shipping point on the Santa Fe line. The town developed in 1882 after the Santa Fe Railroad built the main line across northern Arizona. A grove of ash trees along a usually-dry creekbed gave the town its name. Located on the Colorado Plateau, Ash Fork lies about 50 miles west of Flagstaff in the gentle, rolling foothills near Bill Williams Mountain.

A westerly wind blows incessantly across the plateau. Old timers used to say that, when the town was founded, Ash Fork was 40 miles east of Kingman. Today, it's some 100 miles to the east. Town folks blame the stretched distance on the wind. Oracle Charlebois, the town sage, predicts that by the middle of the 21st century, Ash Fork should be somewhere in New Mexico.

During the years I lived there, 1947 to 1955,

the population stayed about the same — a woman would have a baby and a man would leave town.

Ash Fork may be the only Arizona town that's never been featured in *Arizona Highways*. A rumor has it that Arizona officials once considered a trade with California — Ash Fork for Barstow. No one around town thought that would be a fair deal. Locals thought California should throw Bakersfield in on the deal.

Tourists passing through used to say Ash Fork wasn't the end of the world, but if you stood on your tiptoes, you could see the end of the world from there. There's two things people wanted to get through in a hurry — puberty and Ash Fork.

A good deal of Ash Fork's operating revenue came from handing out speeding tickets to motorists as they fled through town. Cars with Oklahoma or

Arkansas license plates were exempted since they didn't have any money. Everybody else, especially Californians, was considered fair game.

Pundits have called Ash Fork a jerkwater town. I should point out that the term "jerkwater" comes from the old days when the steam locomotives ran out of water in some town that didn't have a water tower. The crew had to grab buckets and "jerk" water from the local wells. Any town that was too small to have a water tower was referred to as a jerkwater town. Ash Fork had two water towers, but it didn't have any wells. All the water had to be hauled in by train each day from Chino Valley, about 30 miles south of town.

Water was expensive, too. Nobody could afford the luxury of planting flowers or grass. Most residents either decorated their yards with huge chunks of flagstone or just left them to the tumbleweeds. Most of us bathed every day, but we changed the bathwater only once a week.

They used to say whiskey was cheaper than water in Ash Fork. That may explain why there were so many saloons in town.

During the election campaign of 1948, the county recorder down in Prescott called the local magistrate, Ash Fork's only elected official, and asked how many voters did they have, broken down by sex.

"None that I know of," Judge Jake Slamer replied with a straight face. "Our main problem here is alcohol."

Ash Fork was such a small town that, by the time the caboose pulled into the station, the locomotive was already out of town.

The town didn't have a fire truck, just a hose. They set up a large mirror next to it so it would seem larger.

The biggest industry was Rowena Lumpkin, the 400-pound Avon lady.

Old Route 66, John Steinbeck's "Mother Road," was a two-laner that ran right smack through the middle of Ash Fork. It was the only paved road in town. On the street above the business district stood a row of look-alike company houses, owned by the Santa Fe Railroad. They were occupied by the muckety-mucks who worked for the railroad, those who didn't have to wear those funny bib overalls. Most of the other houses were small, made of wood or flagstone that was quarried nearby. The side streets were all coated with red cinders and the sidewalks were mostly made from chunks of flagstone.

The town was the butt of many jokes. We took a lot of flak from residents of large cities like Williams, Prescott, Flagstaff — even Peach Springs.

They used to say things like, "Ash Fork is so small they had to share their one horse with another town."

Or, "One year, Ash Fork had a flu epidemic, and nobody got it."

Or, "Ash Fork High School is so small the driver education class and sex education class are taught in the same car."

Even the newspapers poked fun at Ash Fork. A big hailstorm and tornado hit the town in August 1951. The Williams newspaper heralded the event in a headline the next day: "Big Storm Hits Ash Fork — Does $100,000 Worth of Improvements."

Folks were so poor they couldn't afford laxatives for their kids. When one suffered from constipation, Doc Pringle would sit them on a pot and tell scary ghost stories.

We didn't know we were poor until some social workers from Prescott came to town and informed us that being called "poor" was bad for our self-esteem and that henceforth we'd be known as "impoverished."

About six months later, someone from Phoenix told us that our situation was being changed to "underprivileged."

Not long after that, another social worker from the state notified us that we would have to be re-classified as "deprived."

Finally, a federal social worker heard about us and determined that we were "economically challenged."

In the end, we were still poor, but we had a greatly expanded vocabulary.

If those social workers hadn't told us otherwise, we would've never known our plight. Really, we thought we had it pretty good. One time, the social workers took our high school history class to the Phoenix Art Museum to gather in some culture. In the museum was a huge painting of Adam and Eve in the Garden of Eden. Several tourists were standing around the painting. One was a Russian.

"See," he said, "Adam and Eve were Russian. They have one apple between them and they're sharing it."

A French woman spoke up and corrected him. "No, no," she said, "Adam and Eve were French. They have no clothes on, and they're going to make love."

Murphy Blanford spoke up from our group. "You're both wrong." he said authoritatively. "Adam and Eve were from Ash Fork. They have no food and no clothes, and still they think they're in heaven."

In other towns, economic problems were serious but not hopeless. In Ash Fork, problems were hopeless but not serious.

Western movies would have you believe the cow towns were the toughest in the old West. Others would argue in favor of mining towns. But there's nary a doubt that railroad towns were the roughest of them all.

Ash Fork was a railroad town, a cowtown, and a mining town. So it combined the virtues and vices of them all. They used to say you could walk a mile in any direction in Ash Fork and never leave the scene of a crime.

In fairness to the locals, much of the crime was caused by transients hitchhiking through town or by bums riding the rails. Still, Ash Fork was boisterous and rough-and-tumble. The parakeets all sang bass, and any cat that still had its tail was considered a tourist. The high school newspaper had its own obituary column, and at the local bowling alley, you had to bowl overhand. The Catholic parish was nicknamed "Our Lady of Perpetual Mayhem." King Kong was considered a sissy. In 1953, town residents voted for a curfew to protect the town's policemen: At 10 P.M., all the cops had to be off the streets.

One time, a couple of Catholic nuns from St. Anthony's (it was ironic that the patron saint of lost things would also be the resident saint of the little parish in Ash Fork) decided to take a scenic ride on one of the ranch roads north of town. A few miles from town, their old Plymouth ran out of gas. They hiked down the road a couple of miles to the Culpepper ranch house and asked Waddie if he could lend them some gas. He didn't have a gas can, so he took an old bedpan and filled it to the brim.

The nuns walked back to the car and were pouring the contents into the tank from the bedpan when the Baptist preacher, the Reverend Elwood Grundy, and a couple of church deacons happened by on their way back from trying to spread the Word to some workers at the quarries north of town.

The reverend looked at the sisters and sighed with admiration, "Now *that's* what I call faith."

Community pride along Route 66 was measured by the success of the local sports teams.

Forty-year-old men ritually showed up at ball games wearing their tattered high school letter sweaters. They had more gee-gaws stitched on them than stickers on a redneck's pickup bumper. For most, high school sports had been life's high-water mark.

Ash Fork High was the perennial doormat of the league. Our baseball team was so bad that we once got no-hit by a pitching machine. When a game got rained out, the town threw a victory parade. We were so hard up for fans that when somebody called the school and asked what time the game was, the secretary would say, "What time can you be here?"

Every small town has its local sports hero, and Ash Fork's was Joe Bob Looney. He was a big, strapping, good-looking kid with dark, wavy hair and an infectious grin. He was generally happy as a flea in a doghouse. Joe Bob lived with his family on a ranch about a mile north of town and was already flanking calves at the branding fire by the time he was five. His daddy, Jake, and Uncle Billy Bob gained local immortality in the 1930s when they bought that steer from Jubal Spitler.

For Joe Bob's 18th birthday, his mother, Hazel, bought a 200-piece jigsaw puzzle in Prescott. After two months, he announced it was finished. He showed it off to Junior Frisby, who said: "That's really great, Joe Bob. How long did it take yuh to finish it?"

"Only two months."

"I've never done one of these before." Junior said, "Is two months pretty fast?"

"You bet it is," Joe Bob replied proudly. "Look at the box. It says, 'From 3 to 5 years.' "

CHAPTER 2

Rock Doodlers: Dumber Than a Ventriloquist's Dummy

Ash Fork billed itself as the "Flagstone Capital of the World." The hills nearby contained outcroppings of colorful sedimentary rock used for paving and construction. It was quarried by miners known locally as "rock doodlers." They were a bunch of reprobates as colorful as the rock they dug. They were also the butt of many jokes, which they usually took with good nature. Locals stole those Oly and Lena jokes from North Dakota and Okie jokes from the Sooner State and easily made rock doodlers the targets.

One joke went like this: The rock doodler's daughter came home from school one day saying, "Dad, I've got a problem . . . I'm pregnant!"

He gave her a shocked look and asked, "Are you sure it's yours?"

Then there was one about the rock doodler who locked his keys in his car, and it took him three hours with a coat hanger to get his family out.

Another story is told about three rock doodlers who went down to Phoenix to apply for a job. The personnel man called in the first one and said, "I'm going to ask you some questions. The first one is what is 2 plus 2?"

The rock doodler replied, "Thirty-seven."

The personnel man shook his head and said, "Send in the next man."

He asked him, "What is 2 plus 2?"

And the man said "Wednesday."

"Send in the next man," the interviewer said.

He asked the third man, "What is 2 plus 2?"

And the rock doodler said "Four."

The personnel man said with relief, "Thanks be to heaven! Would you mind telling me how you arrived at that answer?"

The rock doodler said, "I took Wednesday away from 37."

They were holding the northern Arizona ice skating championships in Flagstaff and found themselves short a judge. Usually they had a representative from the major towns. They asked for a volunteer from the audience, and a rock doodler stepped up and said he'd give it a whirl.

The first contestant was the 10-time reigning champion from Flagstaff. He came out onto the ice and did a quick turn and fell flat on his behind. The crowd was in shock as he got up and tried again. Again he fell. He tried 15 times, and each time he fell down.

The score cards came up. Snowflake gave him a zero. Winslow gave him a zero. Holbrook gave him a zero. Williams gave him a zero. The rock doodler from Ash Fork gave him an 11, out of a possible 10.

The other judges crowded around the rock doodler, angrily demanding to know why he gave the skater all those points.

"Ye gods," the rock doodler replied. "I think he did very well. It's quite slippery out there."

These two rock doodlers, Reuben and Elam, went fishing up near Williams and caught 50 fish.

On the way home, Reuben said, "I hope you marked that part of the water where we caught those fish for next time."

Elam replied, "I did better than that, I put an X on the side of the boat where we reeled 'em in."

"You fool," Reuben said. "We may not get that same boat next time."

A hot-air balloonist became lost flying over northern Arizona one time. He saw Ash Fork down below, so he dropped down to about 300 feet and shouted, "Ahoy. Do you know where I am?"

A rock doodler looked up and replied, "You can't fool me. You're up there in that little basket."

A traveling ventriloquist was doing a show in the Ash Fork school gymnasium. He and the dummy spent the first 45 minutes of his act talking about rock doodlers. Finally a rock doodler stood up and said, "I'm getting fed up listening to you talk about how dumb us rock doodlers are."

The ventriloquist replied, "It's just a joke; it's all part of the act."

"I ain't talking to you," he argued. "I'm talking to that smart aleck sittin' on your knee."

This rock doodler named Dugan was complaining to Lippy the bartender that he came home from work and found his wife dancing with another rock doodler named Hooligan.

"What did you do?" Lippy asked.

"I went into the kitchen and mixed myself a drink."

"What about Hooligan?"

"He can mix his own drink."

You think Dugan missed the point?

The rock doodlers down at the flagstone yard noticed the boss, Harley Wilbur, was leaving work every afternoon about two. One day, just after Harley left, the workers, including Norval Bumpas, followed suit. Norval was a little slow, the kind of guy who took two hours to watch *60 Minutes*. He arrived home and saw his boss's truck parked in the driveway. He peeked in the window and saw Harley kissing his wife, Ruby. Norval quietly slipped away, returned to work, and didn't leave until five.

The next day, after Harley left, everyone took off except Norville.

"How come you're not leaving early with the rest of us?" one asked.

"Because," Norval said nervously, "Yesterday, I almost got caught."

Literal mindedness is another rock doodler trait.

A mailman rang a rock doodler's door and said, "Is this letter for you? The name on it is obliterated."

"No, it's not for me," the doodler said. "My name's Flanigan."

Gilhooley was even more literal. His wife was in the hospital in Williams having a baby. He phoned the maternity ward and asked the nurse how his wife was doing.

"She's doing fine," the nurse replied. "Is this her first baby?"

"No," Gilhooley said. "This is her husband."

Not long after the Gilhooleys' son, Abner, went off to the University of Nebraska, his mama sent him an inspirational letter. The text has been preserved for posterity:

"Dear Son,

"I'm writing real slow because I know you can't read very fast.

"We don't live where we did when you left because your daddy read in the paper that most accidents happen within a mile of home, so we moved. I won't be able to send you the address because the last family that lived here took the numbers off the house for their next house so they won't have to change their address.

"You know that coat you wanted me to send you? Well, Aunt Elva said it would be too heavy to send in the mail with them heavy buttons on it, so we cut them off and put them in the pockets.

"We got a letter from the funeral home yesterday. They said if we don't make the last payment on Grandma's funeral bill, up she comes.

"Your sister Lucy had a baby this morning. I ain't heard whether it's a boy or girl, so I don't know if you're an uncle or aunt.

"That's about all the news around here for now.

"Love, Mama"

When Abner filled out university entrance forms, he listed his parents' names as "Ma and Pa."

CHAPTER 3

Cowboys

The ranges around Ash Fork had some of the best grazing on the Colorado Plateau. Cow ranches were scattered all over that part of Yavapai and Coconino counties. During roundup, cattle were penned in the stockyards north of town. Afterward, the cowhands would gather down at Gummie's Buffet or the Arizona Bar and spend their hard-earned money.

When I was a kid of about 11, I shined shoes on the streets of Ash Fork. Cattle shipping season was always a busy time. Railroaders never bothered to shine their greasy brogans, but cowboys were a better class of people when it came to personal grooming. There was always the matter of manure on their boots, but once you got past the smell, it wasn't too bad.

They'd belly up to the bar, toss down a few, and then wag their tongues, usually talking about horses. It's an irony about cowboys that out on the range, all they could talk about was women, and as soon as they hit town, all they could talk about was horses. Cowpunchers provided most of the colorful stories that grew out of that part of Arizona.

Cowboys have been described as noisy fellers with bow legs and brass stomachs who work from the hurricane deck of a cow pony and hate any kind of work that can't be done from atop one. They love the outdoors, hate fences, respect rivers, and can spit 10 feet into a stiff wind. And they are independent, too. You just throw one of 'em into a river and he'll float up stream. The only way to get rid of one is to cut off his head and bury it someplace where he can't find it.

That description fit a lot of punchers who lived around Ash Fork. One of the most colorful was

Murphy Blanford, who once declared Adam and Eve were from Ash Fork. He was top hand at the 7UP north of town in 1952 when Charley Oates sold it to Milo LeBaron.

Milo was from back East — back somewhere around Hobbs, New Mexico. He was pretty set in his ways and determined to run the outfit his way. He'd heard that the Yavapai County cowboys were about as independent as a bunch of tomcats, so he figured the best way to show who was boss was to be assertive right off the bat. So, on the first day at the ranch, he called Murphy over to let him know how things were going to be under the new regime.

"Murphy," he said, "I'm running this outfit with a tight fist, and I want us to get off on the right foot. I'm a man of few words. When I say 'come,' I want you to stop what you're doing and come."

The cowhand stared resolutely at his new

boss for a long moment, then replied stubbornly, "Boss, I'm a man of few words, too. When I shake my head, that means I ain't coming."

But when he wanted to, Murphy could speak out, like he did during the summer of 1953 when the Snerdly Brother's One-Ring Circus made its annual visit to Ash Fork. The circus had all kinds of exotic critters like bull snakes, roadrunners, and a tattooed lady who also sported a goatee. People drove from as far away as Williams to see the show. Murphy drove into town all excited and grabbed a seat on the front row.

The star of the show was a beautiful lady lion tamer named Flossie. She was wearing a bright red outfit so tight that you could read the factory names on the labels of her undergarments. She had that lion completely under her control. She'd crack her whip a couple of times and then point a beckoning finger at the big cat, and it would meekly come to her and rub its muzzle against her.

Each time she did it, the crowd roared its approval. After the seventh time, Murphy stood up and declared, "That's no big deal. Anybody could do it."

The ringmaster fixed his glare on the cowpuncher. "Well, sir," he challenged, "would you like to try?"

"You bet I would," Murphy replied, jumping to his feet. "But get that lion out of there first."

That wasn't Murphy's first experience with the circus. As a youngster he hired out as a human cannonball with a traveling show. They'd load him in the cannon and shoot him across the arena to a safety net. He was real popular with the crowds but, being a puncher by trade, couldn't stay interested in anything other than cowboyin' for very long. So, after a few weeks, he went up to the boss and said he wanted to quit.

"You can't quit," the boss insisted.

"Why can't I?" Murphy shot back.

"Because where would I find another man of your caliber?"

Murphy was in Scottsdale one night and decided to check out a new tourist bar. It was one of those fancy Gay '90s saloons called the Lulu Belle. When he arrived, the place was crawling with Easterners. As he walked up to the bar, he was met by a bouncer who was big enough to go bear hunting with a switch.

"You can't come in here without a tie!" he insisted.

Murphy walked back to his pickup truck and

searched high and low for something resembling a necktie. The closest thing he could find was his battery jumper cables. He tied them loosely around his neck and headed back to the bar.

This time the bouncer waved him in but cautioned, “Okay, you can go in. But don’t try to start something.”

Another time, Murphy decided to check out one of those new topless bars. He was quite indignant when he got back to Ash Fork, saying, “They’ve got all these girls dancing around with no clothes on, and they wouldn’t let me in without a necktie.”

Waddie and Charmayne Culpepper owned the U Lazy S Ranch east of town. Each summer, they earned a few extra dollars on the rodeo circuit.

She was a barrel racer, and he rode rough

stock. Charmayne had long, flaming red hair and a pair of shapely legs that ran from her hips all the way to the ground.

Waddie was tall and lanky, square-jawed, with a thick shock of hair the color of corn silk. A hand-rolled cigarette hung perpetually from his lower lip. When he talked, it bobbed up and down, never allowing ashes to build on the lit end. He could roll his own with one hand, an art that has all but vanished from the American scene. He'd peel off a paper and make a trough. Then, he'd pull the strings of the Bull Durham sack and spill tobacco into the trough, lick the edges and seal it up — all with one hand. Then, he'd strike a match on the seat of his pants and light up.

At one time, my life's sole ambition was to learn to roll and light a cigarette like Waddie. That dream turned into my worst nightmare the day some of the boys gave me some Red Man chewing tobacco and showed me how to load up. They forgot to tell me not to swallow. I swore off tobacco in any shape or form. To this day, the mere smell of Red Man causes my stomach to heave.

There was a lot of open highway between towns in northern Arizona, and it encouraged speeding. One day, Waddie and Charmayne were heading toward Prescott in their old pickup. They were rolling along near Hell's Canyon when a highway patrolman pulled them over. The officer stuck his head in the window and asked politely, "Do you know why I pulled you over?"

"Probably," Waddie snorted, "because I'm the only one you could catch."

"No, sir," the patrolman said patiently. "I

pulled you over because you were going 75 miles per hour in a 55 zone."

"I was not," Waddie argued indignantly. "I was going 55!"

"Sir, you were going 75!"

"Don't tell me what I already know," Waddie persisted. "I was doin' 55."

"Seventy-five," the officer insisted.

"Fifty-five," came Waddie's stubborn retort.

Finally, Charmayne couldn't stand it any longer. She leaned over and said, "Officer, it ain't no use to argue with Waddie when he's been drinking!"

Hollywood produced several films about going to the moon during the early 1950s. Motion pictures like *Destination Moon* and *Rocketship XM* had everybody talking about a moon expedition. One night after a space movie, Waddie explained to the boys down at the Do Drop In café that some people from Seligman were planning an expedition to the sun.

"They can't do that," Pinky Graveldinger argued. "Why, they'd be burned alive."

"No, they won't," Waddie assured him. "They're going at night."

One time, a tourist stopped for gas at Freddie's Texaco station and happened to notice Waddie filling up a 50-gallon drum with water.

"Where are you taking the water?" the tourist asked conversationally.

"Out to my ranch," Waddie replied casually. "We have to haul all our drinking water."

"How far away is your ranch?"

Waddie swung his head northward saying, "Five miles thataway."

"Wouldn't it be easier," the tourist wondered, "to dig a well on your ranch?"

"Won't make no difference," Waddie shrugged. "It's five miles to water either way."

The Reverend Elwood P. Grundy one time got his car got stuck in a mud hole out north of town and walked over to the Culpepper ranch for help. Waddie hitched up a team of mules and went back with the preacher to pull the car out of the mud. He didn't get back until after dark.

"What took you so long?" Charmayne asked.

"With that preacher standin' there," he said disgustedly, "I couldn't get them mules to understand a word I was saying."

Waddie purchased one of those mules at an army surplus sale and named it "Lazarus." That mule had trouble written all over him, but Waddie kind of liked him. Lazarus would open gates no matter how tricky the knots, or, out of pure orneryness, he'd sit down on the fence and let the stock out. If you tried to ride him, he'd run under a juniper branch and scrape you off. Lazarus had a big US stamped on his rump. One day a neighbor noticed the brand and wondered if the US meant he was one of Uncle Sam's mules.

"Nope," Waddie replied, straight-faced. "That US stands for "unsafe."

A stranger in a store-bought suit approached Waddie cautiously one day, asking "How much is that old mule of yours worth?"

Waddie paused, looking the stranger over real close. "Are you the tax assessor, or has Lazarus been hit by a train?"

One day, a tourist stopped at the U Lazy S and wandered down to Waddie Culpepper's corral during branding, just as the boys were preparing to rope and drag the first one to the fire. "Which side are you going to brand?" the tourist asked politely.

With a straight face, Waddie replied, "Why, the outside of course!"

Late one night, a dusty old pickup truck full of cowboys on a spree pulled into the yard at Dobbin Plunkett's ranch house. In the back were six or seven drunken cowboys singing *Red River Valley* at the top of their voices. It sounded like a whole family of coyotes had descended on the place. Blanche Plunkett lit a lamp and opened the upstairs window. Shorty Roundtree stepped out of the truck. He removed his hat and bowed graciously.

"Is this where Dobbin Plunkett lives?" he inquired.

"Yes, it is," she said impatiently. "What do you want?"

"Could you come down here and pick out Mr. Plunkett so the rest of us can go home?"

Waddie once sold a horse on credit to Dobbin. Dobbin's credit was so bad that people had even stopped taking his cash, but Waddie wanted to get rid of the horse in the worst way.

"That horse is so fast," he boasted, "that when he finally stops, it takes his shadow 20 minutes to catch up."

So Dobbin bought the horse with a promise to pay later. A few days passed, and he stopped by Waddie's, saying, "That horse is fast alright, but he won't raise his head. He goes around all the time with his head dragging the ground."

"Oh, don't worry," Waddie replied. "That's just his pride. He'll hold his head up just as soon as you pay me for him."

One year, Waddie drew a ride on an outlaw horse named Mortician at the Williams rodeo and hardly cleared the chute when that horse started twistin' and sunfishin' to beat the band. Waddie's eyes got bigger and bigger. Then Mortician got to kickin' up his hind legs and caught one of 'em in the stirrup. He started hoppin' around the arena on three legs. Waddie was frustrated as a woodpecker in the Petrified Forest. He jumped to the ground and, with a look of disgust, said, "That does it. If he's gettin' on, I'm gettin' off."

One time, Waddie and his brother Harvey were

out deer hunting in the mountains north of the ranch. Waddie rode in a few hours later leading Harvey's horse. Tied across the back was the carcass of a big, four-point buck.

Harvey's wife, Sadie, went out to the gate. "Where's Harvey?" she asked.

"Oh, he fainted back up the trail a few miles," Waddie said casually.

"You mean to say you left him all alone out there while you brought in this deer?"

"Yeah, it was a tough call," Waddie explained. "But I figured no one was going to steal Harvey."

Another time, Waddie came running into the house and grabbed Sadie, saying, "Come help me. Harvey got bucked off a bronc into the mud."

"Is he in very deep?" she asked.

"Yep," Waddie said. "He's in clear up to his ankles."

"That don't sound so bad."

"Shore is," Waddie replied. "He went in head first."

Waddie was a wiry, rawhide-tough cowboy, not too big, but he was fiesty enough to eat off the same plate with a rattlesnake.

Harvey used to tell of a time when they were teenagers and Waddie wandered into a blacksmith's shop and picked up a horseshoe, not knowing it had just come from the forge. He dropped it real quick and jammed his hand down into his pocket and tried to act nonchalant.

"Kinda hot wasn't it?" the blacksmith asked.

"Nope," Waddie replied, "it just don't take me long to look at a horseshoe."

Speaking of rattlesnakes, Arizona claims its

reptiles are the most potent. Waddie claimed he saw a rattler strike at a rabbit and miss, burying its fangs in a giant cottonwood tree. By the next afternoon, the leaves had turned yellow, and within a week, the tree died.

Waddie seems to be an authority on the potency of rattlesnakes. He was driving a wagon down south into Gila Bend when a rattler struck at one of his horses, missed, and buried its fangs in the wagon tongue. Right before his eyes that tongue began to swell. It was all he could do to get the horses unhitched before the tongue overwhelmed the critters. By the next day, the tongue had swelled to the size of a giant ponderosa pine. Within a week, it was the size of a sequoya. Since lumber was a scarce item, Waddie took a bucksaw and sliced it up into lumber. He had a stack high enough to build him a large ranch house. But the swelling eventually went down, and one day, Waddie came home from roundup, and his house had shrunk to the size of a small condominium and was still shrinking. Eventually, Waddie had to move back into his small rock house and convert his former mansion into an outdoor privy.

A team of boxers from the mining town of Jerome were in town one day to put on an exhibition. The heavyweight on the team boasted he was the strongest man in Arizona, bar none. Pinky told him to go talk to Waddie before he laid claim to that. Unable to resist the challenge, the strongman rented a horse and rode to Waddie's place for a showdown. He rode into the corral where the cowboy was branding calves.

Getting down off his horse, he shouted, "Hey, cowboy. I've been looking for you. They say over in town you're the strongest man in these parts. They say you're so tough you floss your teeth with barbed wire, but you don't look like much to me."

Waddie didn't say a word, just slapped him around a bit, then picked him up and tossed him over the fence. The muscleman landed in a pile of dust. He looked like he'd crawled through a barbed wire fence to fight a bobcat in a briar patch. When he recovered sufficiently, Waddie asked, "Is there anything else I can do for you?"

"No, I guess not," the strongman said meekly. "But would you be good enough to toss me my horse?"

During branding, it's customary to fix up a feast for all the hands when the work's all done. The meal is likely to be a delicacy known around Arizona ranches as Rocky Mountain Oysters. Up in buckaroo country, the same thing is referred to as "calf fries." There was a Nevada cowboy named Charlie Oakes working on the Culpepper outfit during roundup one year when they hired a Frenchman to do the cooking. The fellow hadn't been in America long but was enamored with cowboy life and wanted to fit in. He was an excellent cook and quickly became very popular among the cowhands. On the morning of the fourth day, however, he mysteriously vanished.

Waddie was dumbfounded. The fellow had seemed happy. Knowing cowboys can sometimes play mean pranks, he called the boys together and said, "That new French cook I hired has left. It's hard to find good help, and I want to know what happened."

Charlie studied the skyline thoughtfully. "Well, boss, we don't rightly know. The first day of roundup, he asked what we wanted for noon meal, and I said, 'How about some calf fries?'

"He asked what they were, and I told him. '*Oui*,' the Frenchman said, 'I can fix those.'

"The next day, he asked the same question, and I said, 'Let's have sheep fries.'

"He asked what they were, and I told him. He said '*Oui*, I can fix those,' and he did.

"On the third day, he asked again, and I said, 'French fries!' Well, his eyes got real big, he peeled off that apron, and he high-tailed it out of here. We ain't seen him since."

An insurance salesman from Prescott was out at Waddie's ranch one day trying to sell him some insurance.

"Have you ever had any accidents?" he asked.

"No, I ain't had any accidents," Waddie

replied, "but three years ago a bronc kicked me in the shin and broke my leg in six places. Then six months ago, some danged mama cow stuck me in the ribs with her horns in gratitude after I pulled her out of a bog hole. And there was the time a rattlesnake bit me on the foot."

The insurance agent was puzzled. "Wouldn't you call those accidents?"

"Hell, no!" Waddie insisted. "They all done it on purpose!"

Waddie drew a bronc to ride at the 1953 Williams rodeo that was a bad one to buck. He and that sunfishing brute went on high together, but they came down separately. Waddie returned to earth executing a perfect swan dive into the arena mud in something less than eight seconds. Had it been a gymnastics event, Waddie probably wouldn't have finished in the money either. He started his dive looking good. He went up on high, arched well, but came down flat on his back. Doc examined him the next day and said to his wife, Charmayne: "I don't like the way your husband looks."

"Neither do I," Charmayne deadpanned, "but he's handy around the ranch."

One of those government bureaucrats came to Ash Fork to make sure the ranchers were paying proper wages. He drove to the Culpepper outfit to ask Waddie some questions.

"Mr. Culpepper," he said, shuffling some papers, "the government needs to know if you're paying minimum wages to your employees."

Waddie sized up the government man real fast and said, "Oh, they do, do they? Well, you see that cowpuncher over there? He gets $200 a month just to sit on that horse and watch the cows. He spends most of the winter sitting around the pot-bellied stove in the bunkhouse."

Then he pointed to the haystack. "That's my son over there forking hay. He gets $100 a month and works about an hour a day, then goes into town and shoots pool or plays the pinball machine."

Waddie nodded to the cook shack. "Cookie over there gets $300 a month to cook, but he spends most of his time reading romance novels."

The bureaucrat smiled and asked, "Is anybody else working around here?"

"Just some half-wit who works 18 hours a day and makes about $10 a week."

The government man adjusted his bifocals and asked, "Who is that person? I need to speak to him."

"You are."

Harlan and Annabelle Gunkel were discussing his will at a family dinner.

"I'm leaving my money to you," he said. "But the ranch house is going to the kids. I don't want a worthless sumbitch toasting his shins around my fireplace."

Annabelle scoffed, "What makes you think I'd marry *another* worthless sumbitch?"

Clancy Osborn grew up on a ranch near Ash Fork and was a good enough rodeo hand to win himself a scholarship to Arizona State University. He made enough money at jackpot ropings to pay his way through college, where he majored in agriculture. When America began its quest for the moon in the 1950s, he was one of the first to apply, claiming he'd spent enough time in space while riding them broncs to qualify for the space program, which he eventually did.

He made his first journey to the moon with a monkey. They were given sealed instructions to open when they arrived.

As they approached the moon, the monkey opened his instructions. He was told to steer the space ship into an orbit. Next, he was to get into the lunar landing craft, separate from the mother ship, fire the rockets, and slowly descend to the moon. Then, he was to fire the rockets again and land the craft. He would get out, gather scientific data and moon rocks, get back into the craft, fire the rockets, dock on the space craft, and pilot it back to earth.

Clancy opened his instructions. They said: "Feed the monkey."

Actually, Clancy did get to perform more important functions on a later moon landing. He was on one of the Apollo missions that landed on the moon to pick up specimens. He gathered 27 sacks of moon rocks. When he got home, he sent samples to all the major universities.

Later, Clancy got this angry letter from the head of the astrophysics department at the University of Arizona bitterly complaining that he didn't get any moon rocks.

"I'll take care of this," Clancy said. He went out into his cow pen and shoveled up a bucket of manure, mixing it with rocks, gravel, and dirt. He boxed it up and shipped it to the professor in Tucson.

The professor studied and analyzed the material for four and a half years before sending Clancy a letter saying that, beyond all reasonable doubt, the cow did jump over the moon.

CHAPTER 4

Oracle & Friends

I was shining shoes one day down in Cisco's barbershop where Oracle Charlebois liked to spin his yarns. He was the self-appointed town sage and could color up a story redder'n a Navajo blanket. Nobody could pronounce Oracle's last name, so they called him "Charley-Boy." His father was French and his mother was a Cherokee from Oklahoma. Cisco claimed Oracle was half-Aztec, only he pronounced it "half-ass-tec." Oracle had that classic Indian face with high cheekbones and Roman nose and claimed he was the model for the buffalo nickel. Cisco blew that one out of the water when he produced a buffalo nickel that was coined before Oracle was born. Despite his propensity for prevarication, he was also a pretty good cowhand.

Charley-Boy said that when he was a kid, there wasn't enough water in Ash Fork for drinking during the week, so each Monday, his mother would give him a small stone to put in his mouth and he sucked on it until Friday. By then, he'd sucked all the moisture out. As proof, he'd always pull a small pebble out of his pocket and flash a big grin that revealed several missing teeth.

Since Charley-Boy spent most of his waking hours in the Arizona Bar, it was a pretty good bet he hadn't had a drink of water since Roosevelt was president. Teddy, not FDR. His stories were usually worth believing — up to a point anyway. He'd lead you down the path of plausibility, and you'd have to figure where to get off.

Oracle pictured himself as a wise old guru and dispensed homespun philosophy to anyone who would listen. He was always dispensing wisdom that seemed to have some esoteric, deep, hidden meaning. He'd say things like, "When you buy a cured ham, what did it have?"

Or, "Do one-legged people lose all their socks in the laundry?"

Another time, he sagely declared, "Mason-Dixon knew where to draw the line!"

One day, he was sitting in Cisco's barbershop, reading the newspaper. He put it down and after a long pause said he wished the country would stop blaming Washington for everything that went wrong, since "that great feller died in 1799!"

No one knew for certain whether Oracle ran deep, or, if brains were gasoline, would he have enough to prime a motorscooter? But he could dispense philosophy. One day he was sitting on a bench in front of Freddie's Texaco gas station, whittling on a stick. He looked up and saw an old car, with an Oklahoma license plate, occupied by a tired-looking man, a faded wife, and enough kids to start a public school. Their clothes were as ragged as a sheepherder's britches. About that time, a bunch of rowdy cowboys whooppeed out of the Arizona Bar. He sized up the situation and reckoned, "If them Okies are the grapes of wrath, them cowpunchers must be the wrath of grapes."

Oracle claimed to have house-trained his dog, Spot, (that was back before people started giving human names to dogs) by having the canine lift its leg over the toilet. According to Charley-Boy, Spot could also flush the toilet with his paw. I never thought to ask him what Spot would do if the bathroom door was closed when he needed to go, or what would he do if the lid was down. I'm sure, though, Charley-Boy would have had an answer.

One time, Oracle came home and found Spot running around the yard with Rowena Lumpkin's pet rabbit, Flopsy, in his mouth. Flopsy was covered with dog spit and mud, and he was dead as a doornail. Oracle was beside himself. He didn't have the heart to tell Rowena that Spot had killed her rabbit, so he took the carcass inside and washed it with soap and water, then dried it with a hair dryer (no pun intended). He got Flopsy looking as good as he could and, after dark, put him back in the hutch.

A couple of days later, he ran into Rowena and she said, "I guess you heard we had a death in our family."

"No, I didn't," Oracle lied. "What happened?"

"Flopsy died," she replied, "and the weirdest thing happened. We buried him in the backyard and somebody dug him up and put him back in his cage."

Oracle Charley-Boy and Miguel Aragon

fancied themselves as great outdoorsmen. They went fishing up behind Stone Dam and came back with a real fish story. Naturally, by the time they told the story, the fish had already been eaten, but Oracle swore the fish was so large that they took a picture of it and when they had the film developed, the negative weighed 3 pounds.

Oracle also included baseball as one of his skills. He said he played for the St. Louis Cardinals back in the 1930s. He once pitched nine innings in a driving rainstorm, and the ball never got wet. Or so he claimed.

Oracle also spun a bear tale about when he was near Tonto Creek and met up with a monstrous grizzly. Oracle's horse bucked him off in some scrub oak and headed for the corral. Oracle saw the bear coming on a run, so he took off as fast as his legs could carry him. He ran right up the Mogollon Rim, but every time he looked back, the bear was gaining on him. The forest started to thin out, and somewhere south of Winslow, Oracle started getting winded. He looked back, and the bear was still coming. Up ahead, he noticed only one tree left, and it was about a mile away. The nearest branch was more than 10 feet off the ground. Oracle knew he was going to have to make the jump of his life to catch that limb.

Oracle would pause until the inevitable question came. "Did you catch the limb?"

Oracle would reply, "I missed it on the way up, but by gosh, I caught it on the way down."

CHAPTER 5

Do Drop In

Every small town has a Do Drop In café, and Ash Fork was no exception. The café was so small, you couldn't cuss out a cat without getting hair in your mouth. But it had a cozy, friendly atmosphere, especially in the winter when there was snow on the ground. There were only six booths and a coffee counter. Here, locals, including merchants, cowboys, railroaders, and highway patrolmen, exchanged gossip. During morning rush hour, the tiny restaurant was a mad house. The sound of conversation and dishes clattering was noisier than three jackasses in a tin barn.

The café's specialty was chili so hot that it would burn calories while you were eating it. The coffee was so strong, according to a café advertisement, it would keep you awake three days after you died.

The chef was an ex-army cook named Spike.

His specialty was gourmet Spam and an acronym delight called SOS. He always wore an olive drab undershirt, and his large arms displayed several tattoos of island girls in various stages of undress. Locals claimed he flattened hamburger into patties by squashing them with his underarms. If that was true, Oracle said, he was afraid to ask Spike how he made holes in the doughnuts.

The main attraction at the Do Drop In, at least for all the red-blooded males, was Crystal LeDoux. She was undoubtedly the most beautiful woman to ever take up residence in Ash Fork. I had a big crush on her, but always from a distance.

Crystal had short, thick, naturally curly hair the color of Alaskan gold and skin the tint of pure mesquite honey. Her face was heavenly, with full lips and large brown eyes. As wild as she seemed, there was a sweet innocence in her that melted men's hearts. Imagination is a wonderful thing. Fully clothed, she was sexier than those aborigine girls in the dog-earred copies of *National Geographic* magazine at the school library.

Crystal was first runner-up in the Miss Arizona contest in 1948, narrowly beating Miss Yuma County when the latter's tractor broke down during the talent competition. After graduating from high school, Crystal moved to Phoenix, where she fell in with a fast crowd that cruised Central Avenue in bright-colored convertibles. She was kind of a slow-talking girl in those days, and by the time she got through saying she wasn't that kind of girl — she was.

An instant hit with the cowboys, rock doodlers, and railroaders, she moved around the restaurant with regal grace, swishing her hips and making big tips. She'd casually drop the small change in her apron pocket. Dollar bills were tucked with great flourish inside one of those lacy French bras she always wore. You never saw so many cowboys leave a dollar tip for a nickel cup of coffee. Her other specialty was singing popular country-cheatin' songs like *I Still Miss My Man, But My Aim Is Getting Better.*

One morning, old Doc Pringle, the town doctor, was sitting at the counter saucerin' and blowin' his coffee. He looked up at Crystal and said, "What keeps those buttons on the front of your dress from poppin' open?"

Crystal gave him a winsome smile and replied, "Only your age, Doc. Only your age."

Crystal was a natural athlete. Somewhere along the line, she'd taken up golf and won championships in Williams, Flagstaff, Winslow, and Holbrook. Doc declared her the inter-course champion of northern Arizona. When she heard about that, she laughed for 10 minutes. Only her pal Doc would have gotten away with that one.

Cowboys would ride horseback 20 miles into town just to watch Crystal lean over to pour a cup of coffee. They'd compete with each other trying to make some clever remark that would evoke a smile from her. She took it all in stride and always seemed to have a quick comeback. One afternoon, when she was the only waitress on duty, the place got busy real sudden, filling with cowboys, along with a few tourists. Over in one corner, the jukebox was vibrating to the wailing, nasal sounds of Webb Pierce singing *The Man From the Gas Company Turned My Woman On*.

Crystal was working her tail off trying to keep

up, taking orders and pouring coffee. She walked up to a table to take an order, and some drifting cowhand looked up and said, "It's been five years since I came in here."

"Well, don't blame me," she said. "I'm going as fast as I can."

Another customer strolled up to the counter and asked, "How late do you serve breakfast?"

She smiled sweetly and replied, "Anywhere from 10 minutes to a half an hour. Depends on which waitress you get, and how busy it is."

One time, the Prescott lawyer, Peter Canelo, was in town making his rounds. He used to drive up and down Route 66 looking for car wrecks. He kept a stack of business cards and brochures on the dashboard right next to his St. Christopher statue, just in case he found someone needing to sue somebody. His motto was, "You don't need a reason to sue somebody."

He sat down at the counter and, in his best Clark Gable voice, said, "Hey, honey, where have you been all my life."

Crystal gave him a bored look and replied, "Most of it, I wasn't even born."

Tony DeAngelo, a salesman from Flagstaff, was another recipient of Crystal's rapier wit. He considered himself the most suave and debonair young Casanova on the Colorado Plateau. His black, wavy hair was all slicked back, and he had on a neat, tight-fitting suit and a pair of those patent leather Gucci shoes. His favorite *modus operandi* for picking up girls was reading palms. He also was into astrology.

"What's your sign, baby?" he smiled, flashing two neat rows of white, even teeth.

Crystal promptly extended the middle finger on her left hand.

Tony wasn't smart enough to know when it was time to quit. Next, he asked if she'd like to go to his place after work.

"Why, yes," she said, "I'd love to, but do you think both of us could fit under that rock?"

"Then let's just get in my car, go out to the boondocks, and get it on."

She paused a moment and replied sweetly, "My awareness of your proclivity towards the esoteric aspects of physical behavior precludes such an erotic confrontation."

"I don't get it," he said.

"That's right," she replied.

Crystal usually came out ahead in these *tête-à-têtes,* but not always.

One day, Bubba Clampett and Waddie Culpepper sat down at the counter.

"What'll you have?" Crystal asked.

Bubba looked up from the menu and casually replied, "I think I'd like a quickie."

Crystal looked at him sternly and said, "Bubba, you'd better learn some manners. Now, I'll ask you again, what'll you have?"

Bubba looked puzzled and again he asked for a quickie.

This time she jerked off his porkpie hat and swatted him on the top of the head. Bubba couldn't figure why she was attacking him that way. All he'd done was ask for a quickie.

Finally, Waddie diffused the situation when he said, "Crystal darlin', I think Bubba wants to order the *quiche*."

Pinky Graveldinger was the local handyman. He lived in a tumbledown shack on the west end of town next to the town dump.

One day, Crystal asked Pinky where he bathed.

"In the spring," he replied.

"I didn't ask when," she said, "I asked where?"

He'd come in to tell her about his newest acquisition, a pet billy goat.

"Where you going to keep him?" she asked.

"Oh, I'll keep him in the house."

"Aren't you afraid of the smell?"

Pinky shrugged his shoulders and replied, "He'll just have to get used to it."

One cold winter afternoon Pinky was having a cup of coffee and listening to the jukebox when three tough-looking bikers came in, sat down, and ordered burgers and fries. They were all decked out in their leather jackets and caps — three Marlon Brando *Wild One* wannabees.

Crystal was waiting tables. One look at that gorgeous blonde inspired the bikers to put on a show of macho. They began taunting Pinky about one thing or another. He took the abuse silently, then quietly paid for his coffee and left.

One of the bikers grinned at Crystal and said, "He ain't much of a man, is he?"

She smiled, poured herself another cup of coffee, then looked out the front window and said, "No, and he ain't much of a driver, either. He just backed his truck over three big motorcycles."

Winburn Smith, a regular at the Do Drop In café and owner of the local merchantile store, was mighty proud when his son, Charlie, went off to the state college at Tempe in the fall of 1954.

On his first night on campus, Charlie got into a poker game with a bunch of veterans attending on the GI Bill and lost his entire poke. But Charlie was a resourceful lad with a fertile mind. He called his daddy the next day, informing him that the college was so great they even had a class that could teach dogs to read. It just so happened Winburn had an old hound dog named Blue.

"I know you're crazy about that dog, so why don't you send him down here so he can learn to read?" Charlie asked. "It only costs $1,000 for the class."

Winburn thought that was a great idea, so he wired Charlie the money and sent ol' Blue down on the Santa Fe Railroad.

About six weeks later, Charlie was broke again, this time from betting on the football games. So, he called his daddy again.

"How's ol' Blue?" Winburn asked. "Is he learning to read?

"That dog is reading everything from Plato to Hemingway," Charlie said enthusiastically. "Now, the college wants to teach him to talk. And, best of all, it'll only cost another $1,000."

Winburn also thought that was a great idea, so he wired more money.

Just before Christmas vacation, Winburn called his son wanting to know how ol' Blue was doing.

"He's doing great," Charlie said. "That hound dog reads and talks just like a college student."

"That's wonderful," Winburn said. "When ol' Blue gets home next week, we're goin' to have a big celebration. Everybody in town will want to come. The high school band will play, and ol' Blue can address the crowd."

Now, Charlie wondered how he was going to

get out of this mess? Suddenly, a light bulb appeared above his head. He hadn't been going to college all these months without learning something.

Charlie and ol' Blue boarded the train at Phoenix, bound for Ash Fork, and somewhere out in the middle of nowhere, Charlie picked up ol' Blue and tossed him off the train.

When the train pulled into Ash Fork, a large crowd had gathered. The first words out of Winburn's mouth were, "Welcome home, son — where's ol' Blue?"

Charlie grabbed his father by the arm and led him aside. "Daddy," he said, "can I talk to you in private?"

They stepped out behind the Harvey House.

"It's like this, Daddy. Ol' Blue and me was on the train. I was shaving and he was reading the *Wall*

Street Journal. Suddenly, he looked up and asked, "Do you think your mama knows your daddy is still fooling around with that waitress who works at the Do Drop In café?"

Before Charlie could utter another word, Winburn grabbed him by the collar and said, "Son, you did throw that lyin' son-of-a-gun off the train, didn't you?

CHAPTER 6

Arizona Bar

The Arizona Bar provided most of the live entertainment in town. On Saturday nights, it was noisier than a pen full of baby calves. Along with her job as the Avon lady, big Rowena Lumpkin was the regular piano player. She was two ax handles wide across the beam. Her backside overwhelmed the tiny piano stool and hung down ignominiously on both sides. You had to use a diamond hitch to keep her on the seat. When Rowena walked across a room, the radio skipped. She got in a rowing machine one time and it sunk. Oracle claimed she sold the elastic from the waist of her worn-out panty hose for bungee cords.

Rowena took up the whole stage, beating out honky-tonk songs, her voice sounding like a burro with a bad cold. She wore a pair of thick, horned-rim glasses with sequins. Her usual outfit was a light blue, flat-brimmed cowboy hat with pink glitter glued to it and one of those embroidered shirts with lots of flowers and fringe on it. She wore tight pants that matched her shirt and hat. The pants fit as tight as a mariachi's trousers. From the rear, she looked like a strolling baby elephant.

Occasionally, the boys would coax Crystal up on the stage. After fortifying herself with a couple of tequila shooters, she could belt out a song with the best of 'em. The one requested most was a popular song out of Nashville called *If I Had It To Do All Over Again, I'd Do It All Over You.*

Proposition bets were a big item at the bar. Once, Pepper Martin, who weighed about 130 pounds, stood up and declared, "I'll bet you 50 bucks I can push something in a wheelbarrow for one block and you can't wheel it back."

The pipeliner looked at him haughtily, slapped

$50 on the bar and replied, “I’ll take that bet.”

The two stepped outside, followed by the rest of the imbibers. Pinky Graveldinger fetched a wheelbarrow in the back of his pickup and wheeled it over to Pepper.

“Now show me,” the pipeliner challenged.

“Okay,” Pepper smirked, “get in.”

The bar was a favorite watering hole for country music singers traveling between Las Vegas and Nashville, and it gave the regulars a break from Rowena, whose entire repertoire consisted of nine songs. The troubadours could pick up a few bucks between the big shows. It also gave the band a chance to practice.

One day in 1953, the word spread around town that country singer John Wesley was coming for a Saturday night. John Wesley, one of the top singers in Nashville, was best known for such classics as *I Can't Get Over You While You're Standing With Him, It Got Around To Me That You Been Gettin' Around with Him, You Caught My Eye Last Night . . . When Your Boyfriend Knocked It Out,* and *I Gave Her A Ring And She Gave Me The Finger.*

Excitement reached a fever pitch. John Wesley was the heartthrob of just about every red-blooded woman in America. And since he was also a top rodeo hand, the men admired him too. Despite the raunchy lyrics to his songs, John Wesley was a straight arrow. According to the fan magazines, he was the manifestation of the all-American country boy: good to his mother . . . had a dog named Shep . . . believed in Jesus . . . drove a pickup . . . and, was a devout family man. For all anyone knew, he still believed in the Easter Bunny and Santa Claus.

John Wesley's impeccable reputation was a

matter of speculation for the barflies. Did he get propositioned by the groupies in every town? Could he resist anything except temptation?

One night, the boys gathered at the bar were discussing John Wesley's virtues and possible vices and, as the discussion heated up, they began to speculate as to whether someone as good looking and sexy as Crystal LeDoux could lead him astray. Lippy, the bartender was particularly outspoken. John Wesley was his hero. He even had a photo of the county singer hanging over the bar, cut off the back of a Betty Crocker cake mix box. He was convinced nobody, not even Crystal, could lead him astray.

"We're all just a bunch of small-town bumpkins," he whined, "and I've got a $100 that says John Wesley would turn her down cold."

Crystal might never have been a party to such

an event, but her pride was hurt, not to mention the fact she'd been drinking Jack Daniels shooters all afternoon with Doc Pringle, something that had loosened her inhibitions considerably.

She slapped down $100 in tip money and called Lippy's bet. Doc slapped $200 more on the bar to back her play. Lippy had started the whole thing and had no choice but to open up the safe and lay down two more $100 bills. The pot was up to $600, winner take all.

Doc was picked to hold the money until the winner was determined. By this time, the side bets placed by the barflies had reached nearly $1,000.

If Crystal had any second thoughts about trying to seduce John Wesley, she kept them to herself. But Lippy never missed a chance to remind her that the Nashville singer had a loving wife and several children waiting at home. He'd stoop to anything to win the bet. He hung another large photograph, this one of John Wesley and his family, over the bar two days before the singer's arrival. It was meant to serve a dual purpose. First, it aimed to remind John Wesley to walk the straight and narrow, resisting temptation; and second, to intimidate Crystal, who didn't ordinarily date married men.

The big night finally arrived. John Wesley came in with his three-piece band, all decked out in glittering sequin suits from Nudie's of Hollywood. Lippy's house band, led by Stem Hobgood, did the warm-up. Halfway through the show, Crystal climbed up on the stage with Stem and began singing some of Texas Kitty's heartwarming hits like *When They Operated On Daddy, They Opened Up Mama's Male* and *I Used To Kiss Your Lips But Now It's All Over*. She sang every song seductively straddling the microphone stand and never taking her smoldering brown eyes off John Wesley.

Lippy, meanwhile, made an effort to bring the family photograph over for John Wesley to autograph. He also inquired as to the health and welfare of John Wesley's wife and children. The mind games going on between Lippy and Crystal had all the makings of a heavyweight prizefight.

John Wesley put on a great show for the folks and during the encore, he called on Crystal to join him on stage. She took advantage of the situation to work her charms once more. Afterward, he asked her to join him for a drink.

A few minutes after midnight, the two of them left the bar and got into John Wesley's '49 Cadillac limousine and drove away.

The next morning, Crystal was waiting at the front door of Doc's office with a big smile, waiting to pick up her winnings. Doc counted out the money and Crystal tucked it in her lacy bra and headed for Prescott.

Nobody ever knew for sure what happened that night. Lippy speculated that Crystal and John Wesley never slept together, but he couldn't prove it. He was convinced she cut a deal with the Nashville singer to take her home for the night, sleep in separate beds, then split the money.

He might have been right. Crystal usually drew the line when it came to dating married men.

Each evening, Tuffy McGraw would drive his pickup into town, pull up a stool at the Arizona Bar, and order four shots of Irish whisky. Lippy, the bartender, was still new in town then, and he watched curiously as Tuffy lifted each one in a toast and sent it down the hatch. The next night Tuffy repeated the ritual, but Lippy shrugged and said nothing. On the third night his curiosity got the best of him.

"Why do you take four shots at the same time?" he asked.

"It's for me three brothers in Ireland," Tuffy replied. "Since we can't be together, I toast and drink with them here in Arizona each night."

Tuffy's ritual went on for several weeks until one night he came in and ordered only three drinks. The next night, it was the same — only three drinks. Lippy asked as delicately as possible if one of Tuffy's brothers had passed away.

"No," Tuffy said. "They're all still alive."

"Then why are you ordering only three glasses?"

"Doc Pringle told me to quit drinking for a spell, as it was bad for me health."

Blanche and Dobbin Plunkett were Ash Fork's closest couple, so close that one night in the

Arizona Bar it took six deputies to pry them apart.

Blanche and Dobbin met at a dance in Williams. Shorty Roundtree, his best friend, later described how they became paired up. “Blanche was sitting on the other side of the restaurant. She had frog legs . . . but the rest of her looked pretty good.

“Then she sent the waiter over to ask Dobbin to dance. He danced pretty good for a waiter.

“She took Dobbin home and introduced him to her father. Dobbin said, ‘I’d like to have your daughter for my wife.’

“Her father replied, ‘What does your wife want with my daughter?’ ”

“We’ve been married 22 years,” Dobbin said one day, “and we’ve never agreed on anything.”

“Twenty-three years,” Blanche replied.”

CHAPTER 7

Junior Frisby and Loretta

The local deputy sheriff was Junior Frisby. Junior was the living proof for why cousins shouldn't marry. As a baby, he was so lazy his mother had to suck his thumb. He graduated *magna cum dente,* by the skin of his teeth, from Ash Fork High School in 1948. Once he went looking for his family tree and when he found it, there were two dogs using it. Junior wasn't the sharpest knife in the drawer.

"I'm confused," he told his mother one day. "My sister says she has three brothers, and I only have two."

One time, he went bear hunting up on Bill Williams Mountain. He drove for three hours up the mountain before coming to a curve and a sign that said, "Bear Left." So he went home.

Junior had a short buzz haircut atop his bullet-shaped head and a body shaped like an oak barrel. He walked with all the grace of an African rhinoceros. His nose had been busted several times and three lower teeth were missing as a result of having been used as beer bottle openers.

He went into the army during the Korean War. When he came home, he applied for a deputy sheriff's position. He drove down to the county seat at Prescott to be interviewed. The sheriff told Junior that before he could be given a badge he had to pass an oral exam.

"Junior," he said, "first, I'm going to ask you some questions dealing with general intelligence, followed by some dealing with law enforcement, and I want you to answer them to the best of your ability. The first question is: What would you find in Ancient Greece?"

Junior answered, "Old French fries."

"Question 2: Name two days of the week that start with the letter T."

"Today and Tomorrow."

"Question 3: Give me a sentence with a noun in it."

"I like an ice cream cone now 'n then."

"Question 4: Who was Joan of Arc?"

"Was she Noah's wife, sir?"

The sheriff rolled his eyes and shook his head.

"Junior, let's skip the rest of those and go on to the ones on law enforcement. What did Batman dedicate his life to fighting?"

Junior looked puzzled, scratched his head for a moment, and answered, "Was it that ugly rumor about him and Robin?"

The sheriff, by this time, had become very depressed.

"You'd better go home and study some more," the sheriff said, shaking his head, "and come back next week."

Junior came back the next week, and the sheriff resumed the oral exam by asking, "Who shot Abraham Lincoln?"

"I dunno," Junior replied.

The sheriff put away his question sheet saying, "Well, I suggest you go home and find out."

Junior got home that night and his wife Loretta June asked, "Did you get the job?"

"I guess I did," Junior responded proudly. "The sheriff's already got me working on a murder case."

Junior and Loretta June lived on the edge of town in a double-wide. The home was mobile, but the three cars parked in the yard weren't. Junior's front yard looked like a perpetual yard sale.

Loretta June was what is politely called buxom. In these times of political correctness, she would be called obesely-challenged. Her dress size was a six, which referred to the number of acres of material required to make it. The only one who might regard her as a "10" would be a shoe salesman. She had short, curly red hair and a mass of freckles. She used to have long hair, worn in a beehive atop her head, but it got destroyed at the Do Drop In café one day when she walked under a ceiling fan.

Loretta June had a high-pitched, whiny voice that was a contradiction to her Louisiana birthplace, where the women usually spoke with French accents that accentuated soft, cultured broad-A tones. She liked a dip of snuff now and then, and she always kept a spit cup in her pickup truck.

Loretta June wanted to shed her image as a redneck by espousing liberal causes. She decided to celebrate Cinco de Mayo but didn't know when it was. She could cuss like a sailor and, when provoked, she could unleash a litany of profanity that would make a muleskinner blush. One day down at the Do Drop In, she got into such a tirade that a trucker walked over and asked her to watch her language.

Junior met her when he was in the army. He was hitchhiking through some small Louisiana bayou town and passed by a carnival that was offering $5 to anyone who'd wrestle an alligator. Junior was about to step in the ring when Loretta June pushed him aside. She jumped on that poor alligator and quickly won two out of three falls. Junior just naturally fell in love and proposed right on the spot — to Loretta June, not the 'gator.

They spent their honeymoon with Loretta June's Aunt Flossie, a venerable old harridan who lived up in the bayous. One morning, Aunt Flossie sent Junior down to the spring with a bucket to fetch some water. He got down there and started to fill the bucket when he saw these two huge eyes staring up at him out of the water. He ran back to the house as fast as he could.

"Where's my water?" Aunt Flossie asked.

"There's a big old alligator in the spring," he replied.

"Oh, he's been there for years. He's probably as afraid of you as you are of him."

"If he's as afraid of me as I am of him," Junior responded, "that water ain't fit to drink."

Before he decided to become a lawman, Junior wanted to be an accountant. When H & R Block decided to open a temporary branch in Ash Fork, he was one of the many applicants. After the interview, Loretta June asked Junior if it was difficult. He said, "No, it was very easy."

She said, "Did they ask you many questions?"

He said, "No, they only asked me one question."

"What did they ask you?"

"They asked me what six times six was, and I told them 42 and got the job."

She said, "But six sixes are 36."

Junior said, "Yeah, that's what the interviewer told me, but I was the nearest."

H & R Block never got around to opening an office in Ash Fork.

Junior was the kind of guy that you could take out of the country but you couldn't take the country out of him. Until he was 18, the biggest city he'd ever been in was Wal-Mart. One time, he had to go to Prescott to attend a two-week training school for new deputies. The county put him up in a motel where he had his first encounter with an indoor toilet. When he got home, Loretta June asked about the newfangled flushing toilets. Junior thought they were all right except for one thing.

"Don't use that long-handled brush they put next to it," he warned. "That danged thing hurts like the dickens!"

Junior was in Phoenix one day, riding in a taxi. The driver said, "Do you like riddles?"

Junior said, "I do."

"Here's one for you," the driver said. "It's not my sister or my brother, but it's a child of my father and my mother. Who is it?"

"I dunno," said Junior

"It's me," said the taxi driver.

"Hey, that's great," Junior replied, duly impressed.

A few days later in Ash Fork, Junior asked Bubba Clampett if he liked riddles.

"I do," said Bubba.

"Here's one for you," said Junior. "It's not my sister or my brother, but it's a child of my father and my mother. Who is it?"

"It's you," said Bubba.

"No," said Junior. "It's a taxi driver in Phoenix."

One time, Junior found himself temporarily on the other side of the law. A game warden cited him for hunting out of season, and Junior's case came up before Judge Slamer. Before proceeding, the judge asked if he wanted to challenge any of the jurors.

Junior looked them over real close and said to the judge, "Yes, sir, judge. I think I can whup that little fellow in the front row."

Catching speeders was Junior Frisby's main obsession. Out on the west end of town was a steep hill. Further west was a sign that said, "Speed Limit 65." Just as the road dropped into town, another sign, partly hidden by a juniper bush, said, "Speed Limit 25."

My first real job was as Junior's partner in a speed trap. I'd stand at the top of the hill looking innocent and watching for cars with Texas or California plates.

When I spotted one, I'd wave my hat to signal to Junior that we had a live one. The town couldn't afford one of those newfangled radar guns, so he'd sit there in his '41 Plymouth and aim Loretta June's hair blower at it. Then he'd haul the driver down to Judge Slamer's five-and-dime store. The judge deeply resented tourists who drove through town so fast they missed the ambiance.

Writing speeding tickets was the major part of Junior Frisby's job description. If you overlook the usual train wrecks, automobile crashes, fights, domestic brawls, muggings, stabbings, and shootings by railroad tramps and drunken cowboys howling at the moon on a Saturday night, Ash Fork was a pretty peaceful place.

A major criminal outrage did occur late one summer night in 1954 when vandals knocked over the outdoor privy behind the jailhouse. The mysterious event made the front page of the next issue of the weekly *Yavapai County Record*, which proclaimed: "Vandals Destroy Toilet At Ash Fork Police Station — Cops Have Nothing To Go On!"

Junior Frisby went down to Cheetum's Curio Shop and spent six months' pay on an expensive pre-historic pot. Pinky Graveldinger asked him if he was certain the pot was authentic.

"It sure is!" Junior exclaimed proudly. "See the writing on the bottom? It says '300 B.C.'"

Junior's prowess with numbers was an inspiration to Bubba Clampett. He woke up one morning convinced that, henceforth, five was his special number. After all, he was born on May 5, 1905, had five children, and lived at 5 South Fifth Street. On his birthday, Bubba went to the race track in Prescott and was pleasantly surprised to find a horse named Cinco running in the fifth race. So five minutes before the race, he ran up to the fifth window and put $500 on Cinco — and sure enough, the horse finished fifth.

CHAPTER 8

Doc Pringle

Doctor Ambrose Pringle was the Santa Fe Railroad doctor. His office was at the Harvey House, but he maintained a dual residency at the Do Drop In café and at the Arizona Bar. His professional code required him to treat all who requested his services. Besides, the nearest doctor was up the mountain at Williams, 18 miles away. When folks had an ailment, they headed for the Arizona Bar. Doc could usually be found in the back booth, slumped over a glass full of Jack Daniels. Office hours were the same as the saloon's, and patients never had to worry about appointments. Waiting was never a problem as one could just belly up to the bar until your turn came.

Doc had a time-honored method of evaluating his patients' ailments. When they described their level of pain, he automatically reduced it by half, unless the patient was a cowboy. When a cowboy described how much pain he was in, Doc always doubled it.

Doc dispensed medicine, usually pills, from the deep pockets of the scruffy black suit he always wore. A patient would explain the symptoms, then Doc would fish around in his pocket and come up with a handful of pills. He'd sort out a few, hand them over, and send the sufferer on his way. One time, he gave Waddie Culpepper some horse medicine by mistake. A few days later, his wife Charmayne found him out in the pasture lifting his upper lip at some mares.

Oracle Charley-Boy said that Doc, before coming to Arizona, lived in Montreal and he drank Canada Dry. He used to bet the barflies that blindfolded he could identify any drink Lippy the bartender might conjure up. Doc never lost a bet until one day Lippy set a glass of plain water in front of him. Doc took the loss very hard, spending the next few days walking around mumbling, "Got stumped by a glass of water." It wasn't the money that hurt, it was his professional pride. Several years later, when Doc died, they cremated his body, and it took three days to put the fire out.

Doc usually was one of the last to leave the Arizona Bar at closing time. One night, the boys were sitting at the bar discussing their favorite subjects — women, horses, and the weather. The evening started going downhill when Cisco Valdez came in, sat down at the bar, and lamented, "I'm having a bad day. This morning I got a letter from *Readers Digest* telling me I'm not a finalist in this month's million-dollar drawing."

"That's nothin'," Oracle said. "I went to see a fortune teller and there was a sign on her window that said, 'Closed due to unforeseen circumstances.' "

Then Murphy Blanford said, "I got up this morning, put on my shirt, and a button fell off. Then, I brushed by teeth and a tooth fell out. I opened the door of my pickup and the handle fell off. Now I'm afraid to go to the bathroom."

Not to be outdone, Dooley Spurlock picked up the cue and said, "Did you hear about the horse that walked into the bar, sat down on a stool, and ordered a drink. And the bartender asks him, 'Why the long face?' "

Then Shorty Roundtree, who never missed a chance to boast about his native state of Texas, followed that up by saying, "Did you hear about the Texan who died and went to heaven? St. Peter met him at the gate and gave him a tour of all the beautiful scenery up there beyond the pearly gates. But, each time, the Texan would say, 'Yeah, we got somethin' better than that in Texas.' Finally, St. Peter couldn't stand it any longer. He led the Texan over to the edge and pointed out Hell down below with its raging inferno. 'Tell me,' he said, 'do you have anything like that in Texas?'

" 'No, we sure don't, the Texan responded, 'but we got some guys in Houston who can put it out.' "

Then it was Waddie Culpepper's turn.

"Did you hear about the time Pinky's dog, Phideaux, walked into a bar and asked for a drink. The bartender said, 'We don't serve dogs in here,' and he pulled a gun from under the bar and shot the dog in the foot. A week later, the door swung open and that dog stepped inside, this time with a six-gun strapped on his hip, and he said, " 'I'm looking for the man that shot my paw.' "

Not to be outdone by his patrons, Lippy the bartender chimed in. "This grasshopper came into the bar, jumped up on the stool, and said, 'Give me a drink.'

"The bartender said, 'Did you know we have a drink named after you?'

And the grasshopper said, 'You have a drink named Larry?' "

"Hey, Doc," Murphy said. "Did you hear the one about the rock doodler who said to the doctor, 'Doc, my mother-in-law is very sick'.

"And the doctor asked, 'What's the matter with her?'

"And the rock doodler said, 'She thinks she's a bridge.'

"And the doctor said, 'What's come over her?'

"And he replied, 'Two trucks and a bus.' "

Then Doc arose and addressed the motley group.

"A horse eats alfalfa and excretes apple-shaped manure," he began, "and a sheep eats the same alfalfa and excretes little round pellets, and a cow eats alfalfa and releases large pies of manure. Can any of you explain the reason for this?"

All he got was blank stares.

"Just proves you boys don't know crap," he scoffed. "Those who think they know everything are annoying to those of us who do."

With that, he jammed on his hat and stomped out the door.

The cool night air put Doc in a better mood, and as he walked toward his black Model A, he noticed a stranded tourist parked across the street in front of Judge Slamer's five-and-dime. The fella explained he had run out of gas and all the stations in town were closed for the night.

Doc told the pilgrim to fear not, that he would siphon some gas from his car and have him on the road in no time. Doc hauled out a rubber hose (known in those days as an "Oklahoma Credit Card") from beneath the seat, took off the gas cap, jammed the hose down into the tank, and began sucking on it.

About that time, Waddie and the rest of Doc's drinking cronies closed up the bar and walked out on the street and the first thing they saw was ol' Doc hunched over the gas tank sucking on a hose. Waddie looked at the boys, shook his head sympathetically and said, "Boy, I hope I never get *that* desperate!"

Doc was always quick with one-liners.

One day in the Arizona Bar, Waddie asked Doc about a dun horse he had recently purchased. "Doc, this horse walks normal sometime and sometime he don't. What should I do?"

Doc spat out a wad of tobacco juice and

replied, "Next time he walks normal, sell him."

"What's a good thing for insomnia?" Rowena asked Doc.

"A good night's sleep," he replied.

After examining a rock doodler named Callahan, Doc said, "I've got some bad news and some very bad news."

"Give me the bad news first," the doodler said.

"You have only 24 hours to live."

"What's the very bad news?"

"I should have told you yesterday."

A small-town doctor like Doc Pringle was often called upon to dispense philosophy and psychology along with medical advice.

An old cowman named Rufus Longacre said to

him one day: "Hey Doc, I've got a problem. My wife and I have sex only twice a week."

"What's wrong with that?" Doc asked his 74-year-old patient.

"My neighbor's the same age as me and he says he and his wife do it every day!"

"Why don't you say it, too!" Doc replied.

Back a few years earlier, when Waddie was about to get married, he went to see Doc.

"Before I marry Charmayne," he said, "I'd like to get something off my chest."

"What's that?" Doc asked.

"A tattoo of Daisy."

Chester Boatright went to Doc and found out he had only 12 hours to live. He went home and told his wife Elsie.

"What can we do to make you happy these last 12 hours we have together?"

"Let's make love," Chester said.

So they did.

"Make love to me again," he said unhesitatingly.

"I can't to that," she replied.

"Why not?" he asked.

"Because," she said, "I have to get up and go to work in the morning, and you don't."

Henry Pruitt came home from visiting the doctor and told his wife Inez he had some bad news. "Doc told me I was going to have to take these little white pills for the rest of my life."

"What's wrong with that?" she asked. "Lots of people have to take little white pills for the rest of their life."

"I know," Henry replied, "but he gave me only six."

One day, Wally Pitts sought out Doc for some advice to the lovelorn. He'd married Millie, 30 years his junior, and the union wasn't going too well.

Doc advised Wally to show more affection, "Love her every chance you get," he advised.

"How can I do that when I'm out in the pasture working?" Wally protested, "It takes me too long to get to the house."

"So take your rifle out with you and when you feel romantic," Doc said, "fire off a round. She's young and will come a-running out to you."

Wally left, saying he'd take Doc's advice. A few weeks later, when Doc saw Wally walking down the street, he asked, "Well, did you follow my plan?"

"I sure did, Doc," Wally said sorrowfully, "and

it worked for a few weeks, but then huntin' season opened, and she took off, and I ain't seen her since."

Lulu Wannamaker, an old-maid rancher, was having trouble with one of her feet and came in to see Doc Pringle. He removed her boot, exposing the horniest, stinkingest foot he'd ever seen. "Lulu, that's the rankest-smelling foot in Yavapai County."

"I'll bet you 25 bucks it ain't," she cackled.

"I'll take that bet," Doc replied.

With that she reached down and pulled off the other boot and said, "That's the smelliest foot in Yavapai County."

Doc paid off on the wager.

Doc and Cisco were discussing the world's problems at the barbershop one day and stumbled upon the subject of overpopulation.

"The way these kids is breeding today sure is awful," Cisco mused. "By the year 2000, there ain't gonna be nothing but standing room only."

Doc pondered that remark for a moment, then replied sagely, "Well, that ought to slow them down some."

Pinky Graveldinger paid Doc a visit in his office at the Harvey House one day. "What's the trouble?" Doc asked.

"I've been having trouble with my kidneys," Pinky replied. "What should I do?"

"Well, the first thing you can do," Doc said, "is get off my good carpet."

Odie Clark was suffering from severe headaches, and Doc Pringle sent him to a specialist in Flagstaff. After the doctor examined

Odie real close, he said, "Mr. Clark, something in your groin is putting pressure against your spine that goes all the way up to your head and causes headaches."

"What can we do about it, Doc?" Odie asked.

"The only cure I can think of is castration."

Odie was mortified but consented to have the operation. Afterward, he was feeling dejected and decided to go out and buy a new suit of clothes. He walked into Babbitt's department store and told the clerk he wanted to try on a new suit.

The clerk looked him up and down and said, "You look like a 44 long."

"That's amazing!" Odie said, "That's my size."

The suit fit perfectly.

"How about a new shirt?" Odie asked.

Again, the clerk looked him over and said, "16-inch neck and 34-inch sleeves."

Odie slapped his side and said, "Right again! How did you know?"

The clerk just smiled. Once again the size was perfect.

"While I'm here," Odie reckoned, "I might as well get some underwear."

The clerk eyeballed him again and said, "Size 36."

"Gottcha that time," said Odie. "I wear a size 34. You're good but not that good."

"No," the clerk said firmly, "you're a size 36. You wear a size 34 and your groin presses up against your spine and causes severe headaches."

Doc Pringle was called upon to perform a variety of surgical procedures. Winburn Smith came in one day and said he'd like to be castrated. Doc talked until he was blue in the face trying to get

Winburn to change his mind, but Winburn was stubbornly adamant. He insisted on being castrated. Finally Doc gave in and performed the procedure. A little while later, Winburn was hobbling stiffly down to the Arizona Bar when he ran into his brother, Elam.

Elam looked at his brother and asked, "Well, how did your vasectomy go?"

Winburn paused and shook his head and looked up as if to see the light bulb that just clicked on above it and declared,

"Vasectomy, that's the word I was looking for!"

Speaking of vasectomies, Willie Lumpkin, the Waterdog King, came by Doc's office one day and said he'd like to get a vasectomy.

"That's a pretty serious decision." Doc said. "Have you talked it over with your wife, Rowena?"

"I sure have," Willie replied, "and she's all for it."

"What about your kids?" Doc asked.

"Yes sirree, Doc," he said, "the kids are in favor, 17 to 3."

Big Rowena Lumpkin fell down one day, causing a 5.1 quake on the Richter scale in California. She was having some chest pains, so Willie took her in to see the doctor. Afterward, while Rowena was getting dressed, Doc walked out to the waiting room and looked solemnly at Willie.

"Your wife's got acute angina," he said.

Willie pondered that a moment and grinned, "Yeah, she shore does, don't she, Doc?"

One night, however, Willie Lumpkin got a telephone call from Rowena down at St. Anthony's

Catholic Church. "I just won the bingo jackpot," she said. "Pack your bags."

Willie was escatic. "Which shall I pack, summer clothes or winter?"

"I don't care," she said. "Just pack your bags and be gone when I get back."

Willie's sister Thelma asked Doc one time if it was okay to have children after 35, and with a straight-face, Doc Pringle advised, "Thirty-five children is enough for any woman."

Speaking of kids, Dooley and Jo Jo Spurlock had spent years trying to get pregnant and Doc was trying to help . . . medically. Finally, he told them, "You're trying too hard. Relax. Don't worry about what time of the month it is. Be spontaneous!"

A few weeks later, Jo Jo came in for another test and sure enough, she was pregnant.

"Did you follow my advice?" Doc asked. He was nearly as excited as she.

"We sure did, Doc," Jo Jo said happily. "Dooley and me were having dinner, and I dropped my napkin on the floor. We both reached down to pick it up, and our fingers touched. Then our eyes met, and sparks flew. The next thing you know, we were underneath the table making love. And that's when I got pregnant."

"That's wonderful!" Doc said. "I'm sure you're very happy."

"We sure are, Doc, except for one thing," she said .

"What's that?"

"Well," Jo Jo blushed, "the manager of Rod's Steak House told us we couldn't come in there for dinner anymore."

One time, Doc advised Biddie Strode's sister, Lulu, that walking five miles a day would improve her health. Lulu was 65 at the time. Now she's 97, and nobody knows where she is.

Doc's buddy, Pinky Graveldinger, was the local handyman. He lived with a three-legged dog named Phideaux, in a run-down trailer house on the west end of town near the dump. He drove an old Studebaker pickup that was perennially loaded with a mixture of tools, empty pop bottles, and various other sundries of junk he'd picked up around town or at the dump.

Phideaux was his constant companion. That dog was the self-appointed guardian of the junk in the back of Pinky's truck. Not that anybody would want to steal the worthless stuff, but it made the dog feel important and gave him a sense of purpose.

Phideaux had the most pretentious name of all the town's canines, who, if they had a name at all, were called "Rover," "Git," or "Hey You."

Pinky bragged that even on three legs Phideaux was so fast he could chase two rabbits at the same time. He also claimed the dog could bark in three languages, French Poodle, German Shepherd, and Pekinese.

One time, Pinky was sitting in the Arizona Bar arguing the dog's intelligence with Doc. "He's the smartest dog in the world," Pinky boasted. He aimed his finger at the slumbering animal. "Watch this, 'Bang, you're dead.' "

Doc snickered, "He ain't doing anything but sitting there."

"See what I mean," Pinky said. "He knows he ain't dead."

Everybody in town wondered about Pinky. Was he a genius or was he a taco short of a combination plate? One day, he walked into the Arizona Bar dressed in his customary bib overalls, T-shirt, and battered pork-pie hat. Looking down at Pinky's feet, Doc said, "Pinky, you're wearing one black shoe and one brown shoe."

"Yeah," Pinky snorted. "And I've got another pair just like 'em at home."

When Pinky first came to town, some of the barflies were under the impression that he was less than bright and spent their idle hours picking on him. Charlie Farcas was sitting next to Doc Pringle in the Arizona Bar one afternoon when Pinky sauntered in for a cold beer. Charlie jabbed an elbow into Doc's side saying, "Hey, watch this."

He walked across the bar toward Pinky, saying,

"I've got something for you." He held out one hand, and in the palm was a nickel and a dime. "You can have one of these. Which one do you want?"

Pinky reached out and took the nickel saying, "I'll take the big one."

As Pinky walked away, Charlie winked at Doc and said, "Ain't he dumb?"

Later, Doc walked over to Pinky. "Say, don't you know the small coin is worth twice as much as the large one?"

"Oh, sure," Pinky said good-naturedly. "I know that."

"Then why do you let them fool you like that?"

"Because, the first time I pick up the dime, they stop playing the game."